INTERESTING FACTS ABOUT THE ANCIENT AFRICAN ART

ART HISTORY FOR KIDS

Children's Art Books

n this book, we're going to talk about ancient African art. So, let's get right to it!

Africa has art forms that are different from other areas of the world. Because the continent of Africa is vast, there are geographic separations among the different people living there. In ancient times, the varied tribes and groups all had unique styles of art. Despite these individual styles, there are a few themes that appear time and time again in different works of African art.

San/Khoikhoi Rock Paintings in Cedarberg Mountains in South Africa.

ROCK PAINTINGS

The very oldest art forms in Africa are the rock paintings. Some have existed for more than 25,000 years. People in ancient civilizations created this type of art inside caves and on the surfaces of rocks. The Drakensberg Mountain Range in the southern part of Africa is a natural gallery of over 30,000 of these paintings. The earlier paintings show daily life, but as time went on, some of the paintings began to show divine spirits in abstract form.

African Instruments.

African Mask.

THEMES IN AFRICAN ART

African tribes didn't use art the way we do today. Their art wasn't usually created to hang on a wall or place on a pedestal in the corner. Much of the art they created was for use in ceremonies or performances. For example, an elaborate ceremonial mask was designed for a religious or social dance. The artists painted their masks using bright, bold colors.

Another common theme in native African art is the human body. A large majority of African sculptures depicted the human form or gods in human form. These sculptures were usually more abstract in design, instead of being based on the way a person's body actually looks. Another common feature that runs across the style of art from different tribes is that African art was usually three-dimensional.

Sculptures or carvings were more common than flat, two-dimensional paintings. Of course, there are exceptions to this rule. An ancient rock painting might have been painted flat on the surface of a rock, but even with these paintings there is often some engraving of the surface.

So in summary, the common themes across different styles of native African art are:

- A focus on the human figure

- Abstract in design instead of realistic

- Generally three-dimensional versus two-dimensional

- Designed for use, not just decoration

- Bright, bold colors on pieces of art that used color

African masks, masks for ceremonies. Kenya.

African carver.

MATERIALS USED IN ANCIENT AFRICAN ART

Most ancient African art that was created in lands south of the Sahara hasn't stayed preserved into modern times. There's a reason for this and it has to do with the materials that were used to create the art. Most of the art the native tribes created was made of materials that would decay, such as wood and plant fibers. Even art made of leather would not hold up centuries after it was created.

Archaeologists are still exploring major regions of the continent. More than likely there will be new discoveries in the future that will give us more details about the ancient art of these tribes.

There are a few civilizations that have been unearthed during archaeological digs. Art from the Sao, Nok, and Yoruba tribes has been found. Art from the Benin Kingdom, from the city of Owo, and also from the region of Mali has been found.

African tribal art figurine.

ANCIENT ART OF THE SAO PEOPLE

Near Lake Chad in the northeastern part of Nigeria, the Sao Tribe made their home from the sixth century BC through the sixteenth century AD. Archaeologists have found over 15 thousand art objects as well as pottery from this civilization. The Sao people were skilled at working with bronze as well as copper and iron.

Copper mask.

The artwork found includes sculptures made of bronze. There are also statues made of terracotta that depict animals and humans. Terracotta, which means *"earth that is baked,"* is a clay-like ceramic material. Jewelry, urns for funeral ashes, and decorated spears have also been found.

Bronze African sculpture of a hyena.

ANCIENT ART OF THE NOK PEOPLE

The Nok people lived in Nigeria from 500 BC through 200 AD. Figure sculptures found from their civilization are some of the oldest discovered south of the Sahara desert. The sculptures depict animals as well as both heads and figures of people. The Nok culture was very advanced. Their sculptures were made of local clay and most of them were life-size. They used geometric shapes for facial features. Some of their sculptures have body parts with exaggerated sizes like giant ears.

Nok sculpture.

ANCIENT ART OF THE YORUBA PEOPLE

A tribe that lived in the ancient city of Ife in Nigeria, the Yoruba people made stone and bronze sculptures and they also created art in terracotta around 1200 AD. Some of their bronze sculptures were unearthed on Jebba, which is an island near the Niger River. They used very sophisticated techniques for their bronze casting process.

Yoruba Gelede mask.

The human figures they depicted showed a wide cross-section of society-young and old as well as healthy and disease-ridden. Their work was much more true to nature and realistic than the work of other African tribes. They sometimes drilled holes into their sculptures so that they could hang other objects like glass beads on them.

The bronze head of Olokun, (divine king or Oni) founder of the Yoruba.

ANCIENT ART OF THE BENIN KINGDOM

The Benin kingdom was located in the southern region of Nigeria. From about 1440 AD through 1897 AD the people who lived there made beautiful works of art from a variety of materials. They used metals such as bronze and brass. They also used local clay, wood, and ivory. Terracotta was a favored material as well. Their art depicted human forms and animal heads.

Bust of an Oba king, Nigeria, Benin Kingdom.

ANCIENT ART OF THE CITY OF OWO

From 1400 AD through 1600 AD, the city of Owo in Nigeria was the capital of one of the city-states of the Yoruba culture. Archaeologists have found sculptures made of terracotta there. During the 17th and 18th centuries, the rulers of Benin imported objects of art from Owo. Their artists were recruited to come to work in the royal workshops of the kingdom of Benin.

Divination Tapper. Ivory staff. Probably produced in the eighteenth century in Owo.

ANCIENT ART OF THE MALI REGION

The inner delta of the Niger River called the Mali region has been inhabited for many centuries. Many sites have been explored by archaeologists and they have unearthed pottery produced from the 12th century to the 16th century. A majority of the artifacts are human and animal figures that have been molded out of clay.

Seated female figure, Jenne people, Inland Niger Delta region, Mali, c. late 13th to 17th century AD

ANCIENT ART OF THE CITY OF IGBO-UKWU

A large number of bronze art objects were discovered in the village of Igbo-Ukwu. Some of the objects have been dated to the 10th century or earlier. Art objects found here were ritual vessels. Many of the artifacts found contain materials that show evidence that the people were trading long-distance with Egypt.

Bronze ornamental staff head, 9th century, Igbo-Ukwu.

Heap of many ethnical authentic masks.

AFRICAN CEREMONIAL MASKS

It would be impossible to think about African art without thinking of ceremonial masks. The mask has always been a part of performance art. Masks were used for religious rituals and social ceremonies. They generally had a spiritual significance. Artists who created masks had special status within the tribe. Their skills were often passed down from generation to generation.

Masks were frequently designed to depict humans or spirit animals. Some designs blended elements of both humans and animals. Masks were often carved from wood and painted with bright colors. Sometimes the facial features on a mask were designed to show specific characteristics. For example, a mask with a very large mouth and chin may have been created that way to signify strength and authority.

In addition to carving and painting, African artists adorned their masks with feathers, shells, and animal teeth or horns. They sometimes used strung beads for decoration and animal hair or pieces of straw to make hair or facial hair.

Antique African mask

Dogon Dancers with Beaded Masks.

TYPES OF
AFRICAN MASKS

There are many different types of African masks and they vary from being extremely detailed and realistic to very abstract with not many details. These masks were made in ancient times and the native people of Africa still make them today.

The most common type of mask is the face mask. Used in dance and music performances throughout the continent of Africa, face masks can be held on the face in numerous ways. Holes on both sides of the mask make it possible to tie it with either a band or a string. Sometimes a scarf or a wig can be used to hold the mask in place.

Dogon Dancer.

Headdress masks are usually created to balance on a base that the wearer places on his head. The native Bambara group, the largest native group in the area of Mali, are known for this category of mask.

Shoulder masks were large and very heavy and designed for the wearer to support on broad shoulders.

Four Dogon Dancers, Masks and Stilts.

Carved from a tree trunk, a helmet mask was designed to fit over the entire head of the wearer. Helmet crests were designed to be worn like hats. The wearer's face would not be covered.

Cap crests, also called forehead masks, would be worn on the forehead leaving the remaining part of the wearer's face uncovered.

Awesome! Now you know more about the style and techniques of Ancient African Art. You can find more Art books from Baby Professor by searching the website of your favorite book retailer.

Visit

BABY PROFESSOR
EDUCATION KIDS

www.BabyProfessorBooks.com

to download Free Baby Professor eBooks
and view our catalog of new and exciting
Children's Books